The

Happiness

Option

By Othello Bach

CHOICE BOOKS

The Happiness Option is an excerpt from *Life After Trauma and Abuse*, by Othello Bach

ISBN-10: 1508580693

ISBN-13: 978-1508580690

Printed in the United States of America

To Those Who Want to Move Beyond

Trauma and Abuse

Table of Contents

Introduction

I know what abuse is. I know how it feels, how it hurts, and how difficult it is to cope with the painful memories.

I know the insulting, demeaning words that echo through your head when you try to act as if you are as smart as... as good as... and as deserving as everyone else—because deep down you don't believe it—and you feel like a fraud.

I know what poverty is, how hunger feels, and how cold your feet become when you have no shoes in winter. I also know the humiliation of facing classmates who point and laugh at your bare, dirty feet.

I know what it's like to be seven years old and watch your mother burn to death then experience terrible guilt because you wanted to save her... to do something to help... but you couldn't.

I know the shame of being taken to your alcoholic father's bed, and the loneliness of being separated from your brothers and sisters for eleven years in an orphanage.

I am also aware of the criminal abuses that take place when children are left in the care of unscrupulous adults— and how easily a young, trusting girl can be raped.

I know because I've experienced these things.

Yet, I *also know* that you can move beyond the devastating effects of an abusive past. I know, because I no longer cry or feel hurt and cheated when I think of these things. The nightmares have disappeared, and the fear that "others will reject me if they really know me" is now a thing of the past.

I no longer doubt my own convictions or see my ideas as too stupid to share, or compare myself to others to make myself feel good (or bad).

I don't need to hide in the shadows or lose myself in a crowd because I think I'm so ugly—inside and out—others will make fun of me.

Anger and resentment no longer make me "fly off the handle," and I'm confident I can deal reasonably with the situations and circumstances I encounter.

The wonderful thing about this is that if *I* can do it, *so can you.* We are not different. Our pasts may vary but the tools we use to carve out a new life are the same, and are available to all of us. Anyone can learn to use these tools to create a happier, more productive, and more rewarding life.

If you will study this booklet and do the exercises, in one short month you'll prove to yourself that you can take charge of your life—no matter what horrors you have experienced.

You can change the way you feel about yourself and the way you respond to others. I've used this method to help hundreds move on and live happier, more rewarding lives.

Perhaps you will become one of them.

Is This For You?

Has some past experience left you feeling as if you have lost the best part of yourself—your innocence and ability to love?

Are you haunted by specific memories?

Do you find yourself so confused and frightened that you silently scream, "Someone, help me!" when there is no one around but you?

Do you occasionally feel as if you are stuck in an absurd play and you don't know your part—and worse, you don't deserve to know?

Are you terrified to make decisions because you might make the wrong one... so you make the same decision you always make in that particular situation? Then, do you hate yourself afterwards because you didn't have the nerve to do what you really wanted to do?

If you have never experienced any of these doubts and fears, then this booklet is probably not for you.

On the other hand, if you have experienced any or all of these responses—and you know the information within these pages is for you—read carefully and slowly. Do not skim, rush, or push yourself. To move beyond abuse requires thoughtful consideration and commitment to someone you do not now consider worthy of consideration: you.

Consequently, there will be a strong temptation to skim, rush, or "push" yourself. This is a common reaction for those who do not like, trust, or respect themselves—a trait well known to abuse victims. Unaware of their deeply held subconscious belief that they do not deserve to succeed, they fail to recognize when they are undermining their own best efforts.

Make sure you understand each point before going to the next. Treat yourself with the same respect that you would treat an abused and neglected child. For instance, you would never tell a mistreated child that "You're hopeless! You'll never get this!" You would never say, "You don't deserve my attention, my time, my concern, and devotion!"

You would, instead, sit as long as needed and repeat as often as necessary the words that would help that child feel loved and worthy of respect.

So do the same for yourself.

When you find your mind wondering back to the abuse or drifting in another direction entirely—recognize this as resistance to your own healing. It is the most common way that you neglect and abuse yourself. By allowing your mind to wander, instead of focusing on the task at hand, you are reinforcing the notion that you are unworthy, and denying yourself the benefit of healing.

Damaged Beyond Repair?

Yes, you have been hurt. No doubt you can remember the fine details of every situation and circumstance in which you were hurt.

Perhaps you believe you are scarred for life. If so, that's good. A scar is evidence of healing. Scars bear witness to past injury. You can remember the initial pain of the injury if you desire, but the injury no longer exists.

Are you damaged beyond repair?

Only if you decide you are.

Scars from past injuries do not testify to "damage beyond repair" but to healing.

What you decide about yourself and your ability to move on is more important than anything that has ever happened to you. And, it always will be.

You are not the sum of your experiences. You are whatever you decide to be. Decisions are made in the mind, and the mind is always free to change and decide again—and again. You may have decided many years ago that you could never be completely happy again, and that decision has stood only because you haven't reversed it.

Only you can decide what you want to do with your life—whether you want to live happily, enjoying yourself to the fullest, or settle for being an abuse victim scarred for life. Whatever your decision, your life will reflect it, just as it reflects every decision you make.

No one can decide for you, regardless of how much they might want to. Parents cannot decide to "make" their children happy any more than children can decide to "make" their parents happy.

Blaming today's unhappiness on past abuse is like blaming today's bad weather on last spring's tornado. The only connection is in your mind.

Today's unhappiness is a result of your thoughts and beliefs today, and primarily those thoughts and beliefs about you. The good news is that *you can change your thoughts and beliefs.*

Happiness is a gift you must give yourself. If you expect someone else to do the impossible—make you happy—your life is already filled with disappointment and misery, and it will remain that way until you decide to assume responsibility for changing it.

You can move beyond guilt, grief, anger, fear, and pain, and create a completely new image of yourself. Your success depends entirely on how determined you are to live a more rewarding life. If you truly want to free yourself emotionally so that you can fulfill your desires and make your dreams come true, there are tools that can help.

Your success will depend on whether you really want to be happy—not on whether you believe you deserve to be happy, because at this point you don't! But as you use the tools laid out in this booklet, you will begin to feel more and more deserving, until at last, you finally give yourself what you really want.

Regaining self-respect

For over 30 years, abuse issues have been addressed in every conceivable manner, and while there are some fine programs, there are others that only validate the pain and help the victim blame the abuser. Validating the pain may be temporarily soothing but it is rarely productive; the victim already knows whom to blame—and no one will ever find self-respect by blaming "the past" for conditions in the present.

Dealing With the Effects

Victims of abuse feel as if they have been robbed of innocence and no longer have control over their lives. This is not true; it only seems that way. When others hurt us, regardless of the reason, they do not actually take innocence or power away from us. However, when we are young and do not know how or why we suddenly feel such a loss, we also do not know where or how to find and reclaim those wonderful feelings.

Almost without exception, when we are victimized as children, we reach erroneous conclusions about ourselves, our relationship to others, and the world. The mere fact that our parents or caregivers treated us with disregard made it easy to reach flawed conclusions, such as: I am not loved; therefore, I am unlovable. I must be a horrible person, but I don't know how to be different. I don't know how to make others love me. I have no control over my life!

Such conclusions quickly became beliefs that sank deeply into the subconscious and have continued to operate as "truths," negatively influencing every decision we have made. If we take no steps to undo these beliefs and remain "a victim," we choose a life that offers no genuine rewards and only meager short-lived satisfactions—most of which are derived from punishing our abusers and blaming others for our unhappiness and failures. Unfortunately, these small "victories" never prompt feelings of real pride and always impede our success.

Moving beyond abuse is difficult but not nearly as difficult as continuing to live as "a victim."

Those of us who experienced childhood abuse generally need help from every available source, but we should never forget that no one can help us more than we can help ourselves. Counselors can educate and inform and act as catalysts for change, but they cannot make us change our minds about ourselves, nor can they reclaim our innocence and sense of power. This is a task that must be performed by every individual sufferer.

Only those who want to move ahead and leave victimization behind will put forth the effort required to succeed, because it takes real effort to replace one belief system with another. It also requires constant vigilance— paying attention to emotions and the thoughts that create them—as well as replacing hurtful memories with ideas that create a sense of value and self-worth.

Moving from a belief that you are a victim to a belief that you are in control of your life means constantly correcting your thoughts and words, and bringing them into alignment with what you want—a belief that you can accomplish anything you set out to do. Old thoughts and words will slip back dozens of times a day when you first begin, but, as with anything else, the more you practice, the easier the task becomes.

Are You Willing?

You cannot be a victim and also be in control of your life. Moving from "victim" to "being in control of your life" means you must be willing to give up the idea that you are a victim. Generally, the very idea of giving up your victim status is confusing and insulting. It's as if you are being asked to do the impossible: to give up yourself—your true identity.

Yet, you were not born with the mindset of a victim. That is a learned response which has become a firm belief. You are much more than a victim, and to allow yourself to continue believing that you are defined by your experiences will only limit the rest of your life.

You are capable of enjoying all the beauty and grandeur that life has to offer and to partake in all of life's sweetest experiences. Yes, it hurt your feelings to be treated abusively. It grieved you to be neglected, beaten, or mistreated. Yes, you experienced terrible pain at the time these things happened, but your mind was not permanently damaged. It works as perfectly now as it did when these things happened—and your mind is the only tool you need to change the direction of your life.

Building "Mental Muscles"

It all begins with mental exercises.

Imagine that a "couch potato"—an out-of-shape observer of life—decides he or she wants to become an Olympic champion. Obviously, it will take greater determination and effort for the couch potato than it would for a healthy, "in shape" person. The same is true for those who have been beaten down emotionally but who truly want to live happy, fulfilling, and productive lives. They can do it, but not without developing the "mental muscles" necessary to succeed.

Mental exercises build "mental muscles" that enable you to get up when you fall, and keep you on track as you develop and implement plans to reach your various goals. Mental exercises are the first important step, because you will need them to "muscle out" the doubts and fears that, otherwise, will destroy your confidence and undermine your resolve.

Mental exercises are specific words and ideas that you repeat on a regular and sustained basis. They are affirmations that restore your belief in yourself and bolster your confidence so you can succeed. A list of exercises will be included later.

Why Mental Exercises Work

Mental exercises work because:

• Every thought creates a corresponding emotion.

• Emotions create conviction—belief.

• Belief prompts action.

• Action produces results.

Action can't also effect emotion Reversley [handwritten note]

Example: As a child, you are repeatedly beaten, and think: I am not lovable. (1) This thought creates painful emotions. The pain convinces you that your thought is true, and you cry. (2) Believing you are unlovable, you shut down your emotions, thinking this will "protect" you, and (3) you modify your behavior according to your belief. Perhaps you withdraw and risk less, or become hostile and more aggressive, but regardless of how you manifest your belief that you are not lovable, you will (4) produce a specific result.

If you choose to shut down your emotions, you will probably be known as "cold" and "uncaring." If you become hostile and aggressive, you will probably end up in jail.

Through this example, you can clearly see that your thoughts and emotions create the outcomes of your life.

This invisible cause-and-effect principle is constantly at work determining everything you say and do. Only by changing the initial cause (belief) can you change the effect (outcome), and the only way to change an unhappy and unhealthy belief is to constantly feed yourself new, happy, healthy thoughts.

Planning Success

Before you can succeed at anything, you must decide what you want to do, and create a plan of action to make it happen. This is true whether you are a victim of abuse or came from a solid, loving background. No one stumbles into success.

Abused children most often grow into adults who have (1) no respect their own ideas, and (2) no confidence they can create a plan for their own success.

One of the biggest stumbling blocks is that they feel entitled to their pain and anger—and they are! What they frequently fail to realize is that they are also entitled to happiness, and it is not possible to hang onto pain and anger and be happy. The issue, then, is not one of entitlement but of choice between opposite realities, that of being a victim, or a happy and successful person.

Overcoming the effects of tragic events is not easy but it is possible, and definitely worth the effort. There is no sweeter feeling than proving your value to yourself—and one way to do this is to ignore the past and keep working toward your goal. Pursuing a goal is exciting and rewarding in its own right, and accomplishing it is indescribably delicious! Also, the moment you achieve your goal, you will realize you haven't been permanently damaged. You will see that you have taken control of your life and achieved your dream—something that couldn't have been done if you were permanently damaged.

Some call this denial, and it is! It is a form of denial that allows you to be happy and accomplish your goals. The alternative is also denial—of happiness and success—and leaves you convinced that you are a helpless victim.

Which would you rather deny? The choice is yours.

Taking Control

To take control of your life, you must take control of your mind. The good news is that you already have the only tool you need to create a new reality!

You have the power and ability to stop thinking of yourself as you did as a child. I'm alone... I'm no good... nobody cares about me... I'm not like everyone else. There are a thousand such demoralizing thoughts and all of them can be recognized quickly because without exception, they leave you feeling depressed, lonely, and victimized. When you tolerate these thoughts and feelings, you are victimized, but you are victimizing yourself! You are repeating ideas that you learned as a child, and are continuing to use them against yourself.

To end the barrage of insults and depressing ideas, you will need to make a list of at least 10 statements that make you feel strong. These are ideas that encourage, strengthen and support you so you can continue moving ahead.

Examples of Encouraging Affirmations

- I can control my life because I can control my thoughts, emotions, and my responses.

- I am intelligent. I can stop abusing myself.

- My life is important. I will make it important.

- I am calm and confident in all situations.

- Everyone deserves love, including me.

- I can devise an intelligent plan for my life.

- I will make a plan to do something I love, and follow my plan.

- Every day I grow more accepting and acceptable, and feel more accepted.

- Every day I grow more loving and lovable, and feel more loved.

Initially, such statements will make you feel as if you are lying to yourself. The tendency is to think, "Who am I kidding? I can't change what I am." Say the affirmations anyway. Make your own list of positive statements. The more you say them, the "truer" they seem to be because repetition of positive ideas breaks down the old belief that you are a failure, and you will begin to see yourself as someone who can be happy and successful.

Looking for a Rescuer

Most abused children secretly wish to be rescued by some benevolent soul who will suddenly whisk them away and make their lives worth living. The thought of this fictitious person is so pleasant that it becomes a wonderful dream, a fantasy relived daily. These children silently and constantly pray: Please, God, send someone to take me away. Send someone who will be kind and make me happy. This burning desire for rescue eventually becomes a "secret belief"—hidden even from the believer—but it is there, influencing every decision. Someday, somehow, someone will come and take me out of this miserable situation, and I will be happy.

Tragically, this desire for a rescuer is carried into adulthood—from relationship to relationship—and always ends in disappointment, tears, and anger. Although the rescuer is always blamed for the failure of the relationship, victims do not escape unscathed. The failed relationship reinforces their belief that they are stupid or unlovable.

Don't be fooled into believing someone else can rescue you!

The idea that someone else will suddenly change the way you feel about yourself is a lie. Your feelings about yourself and your life are based on your beliefs, and no one can change your beliefs about you—except you. Until you do, life is one, long, futile search for acceptance and happiness. Every relationship is strained and eventually falls apart as you turn to lovers, friends and spouses, expecting them to do the impossible: make you happy.

You must become your own rescuer or you will never feel worthy of success.

There is no magic pill, no "perfect" person, and no ideal situation that will erase the negative ideas you have accepted about yourself. Some people will support you more and longer than others, but no one can replace what only you can do. Some situations are more satisfying than others but even a "dream" situation will not erase the negative beliefs you hold about yourself. You must make the corrections.

This may sound like more responsibility than you want, but the alternative is even less desirable: a lifetime of horrible memories and constant defeats.

You have a Power within you that always responds to love—and nothing else. You can pray for love and acceptance and for God to take away your sense of loss, but unless you are willing to cooperate with the Rules of Love, you pray in vain.

If, however, you are willing to cooperate with the Rules of Love—for even 30 days—you will begin to convince yourself that you have complete control of your life. *And...* if you want it badly enough, you can have it.

When you feel unloved, you feel depressed or dispirited because love is an attribute of Spirit. You also lose self-respect and harbor feelings of anger and resentment, guilt and shame. Consequently, it is only when you restore love to your own mind that you begin to feel loved and respected again.

Almost everyone is familiar with the idea that "God is love" (1 John 4:8) but few know how to use this information to their benefit. They pray for help and love but do not know how to actually use love to help themselves.

The Happiness Option (Pg. 27) is designed *to use love* to *restore* love. It is not only for those who have been abused or neglected in the traditional sense, but also for anyone who senses there is more to life than they are presently experiencing.

Within 30 days, it is possible to experience tremendous relief in areas where pain and resentment have had crippling effects for years. A deep sense of satisfaction, purpose, and well-being can be reestablished in that short time. After the initial 30 days, those who have been practicing The Happiness Option can decide if they want to continue until it becomes a *habit*— or return to the habit of creating feelings of loss and victimization.

The Happiness Option

The Happiness Option is a 30-day commitment to practice mental exercises that can change negative beliefs to positive beliefs about you and your role and purpose in life. These exercises were developed and used as the basis for seminars entitled "Life After Trauma and Abuse." They are based on mental and spiritual principles aimed at restoring love and eliminating fear and guilt.

The Happiness Option dramatically demonstrates the positive effects of accepting full responsibility for your thoughts and emotions and focusing your full attention on love.

Anyone determined to experience more happiness and love will find The Happiness Option extremely helpful. It is designed in "steps" that, if followed as directed, will clearly demonstrate your ability to take control of your life.

The Happiness Option can be worked alone or in groups. There are certain advantages to working with a group, such as sharing experiences and finding inspiration in each other's successes. However, anyone who is serious about changing his or her life can do so by working The Option alone.

Hundreds of people who have worked The Happiness Option alone have experienced wonderful effects. So whether you choose to work The Option alone or start a group and share it with others is entirely up to you. Ultimately, of course, it is up to you to do the exercises.

How and Where to Begin

Read through the entire booklet before beginning the first step.

The first day will likely require an hour or two of your time. After that, only a few minutes a day are needed to work the various steps.

You will, no doubt, forget and stumble many times because habits are hard to change. However, if you ignore your stumbles and *decide* to live a happier, more rewarding life, you will succeed with The Happiness Option.

Step 1

(To be done the first day, and repeated every day for 30 days.)

When you are ready to make the commitment, mark 30 consecutive days on a calendar. These can be the most important 30 days of your life. Each day, put a checkmark on that day to remind yourself of your progress. As you check the day, think to yourself, "Today, I choose to be happy." As you think this pleasant thought, allow the expectation of a pleasant day to create a sense of happiness within you.

As the day progresses, stop several times to assess your emotions. If you are experiencing anything other than happiness, try to identify what you are feeling, and say to yourself, "I am feeling (anxious, afraid, worried, angry, etc.) and I prefer to feel happy." Then, once again, remind yourself, "Today, I choose to be happy." Think of something that makes you smile and allow that pleasant thought to create a sense of happiness within you.

Step 2

(To be done the first day only.)

Take one hour or less to make a list of every past painful experience that makes you unhappy when you remember it. No priority need be noted. Make no judgments why this experience should make you unhappy. If it makes you unhappy, put it on the list.

Examples of past pain might be:

- When my mother/father died.

- When my parents divorced.

- When my husband/wife left me.

- When I lost my job.

- When I declared bankruptcy.

- When my best friend lied to me.

- When I lost my diamond bracelet.

Next, write across an envelope the words "Past Pain." Put the list in the envelope but do not seal. You may take five minutes from each day to add to the list any memories that come to mind later. Do not dwell on those memories;

simply add them to the list and then dismiss them. Commit yourself to the idea of leaving these thoughts on this list, refusing to consider them for 30 days.

Step 3

(To be done the first day only.)

Take one hour or less to list every future concern and fear which you can do nothing about. No priority need be noted. A fearful thought creates fear. Make no judgments why these thoughts should frighten you. Fear is fear. Put it on the list.

Examples of future fears which you can do nothing about might be:

- Dying in an automobile accident.

- A spouse or lover leaving.

- Earthquakes, tornados, terrorist attacks.

- A child's sexual preference or orientation.

- A family member's alcoholism.

- What other people think.

- What other people do.

Next, write the words "Future Fears" on an envelope, put the list inside the envelope but do not seal it. Each day you may take five minutes to add to this list if other fears arise. Do not take more than five minutes. Commit yourself to the idea of leaving these thoughts on this list, refusing to consider them for 30 days.

Step 4

(To be done the first day only.)

Take one hour or less to list all the fears, concerns, and worries that you *can* do something about. These are *your* worries and concerns; therefore, *you* are responsible for doing something that will relieve *your* anxieties.

Examples of fears I can do something about might be:

- The car will break down.

- I will lose my job.

- I may not get a certain job.

- I'll never finish school.

- I don't make enough money.

- I'm not a good parent.

- I'll always be alone.

- I may be an alcoholic.

- No one will ever love me.

Next, beside each fear, make a note of *what* you can do to relieve this fear, and *when* you can do it. Leave this list out so you can refer to it each day. Do what you can do, and forget what you cannot do that day. (Also be aware of the difference between "cannot do" and "will not" do. Honesty is essential to your success.)

Your list and responses might look something like this:

- The car will break down.—*I can't afford to take it to the shop, so I'll ask my brother (neighbor, friend), who works on his car, to take a look at it. I'll do that this weekend.*

- I may lose my job.—*I'll be more punctual and more careful. I'll volunteer to work late if the boss needs me. I'll do this tomorrow.*

- I'll always be alone.—*I'll make myself more available. I'll attend office parties and accept invitations from friends who go out in groups to socialize. I'll accept the next invitation.*

Step 5

(To be done the first day and added to frequently.)

Make one last list. Take as long as you like. Write across the top of the page "Thoughts that make me happy." No priority need be noted. Make no judgments why these thoughts should make you happy. If a thought makes you happy, put it on the list.

Make several copies of this list. Put a copy in every room of your house or apartment. Put a copy in your wallet, briefcase, or purse. Put a copy in your car, office, or any other place you are likely to be. Literally, paper your life with this list. Leave yourself no room for deception to say, "I couldn't think of anything happy."

Example of thoughts that make me happy might be:

- Holding my grandbaby.

- Being thin and sexy.

- Kissing my boyfriend/girlfriend.

- Having perfect health.

- Having $100,000.

- Winning an award.

- Lying in the sun in Florida.

- Buying a house.

- Having my husband/wife love me.

- Having my parents' respect.

- Hugging my children.

- Being promoted.

- Owning my own business.

- Receiving a raise.

- Losing 40 pounds.

Read your "Thoughts that make me happy" list several times a day, and as you read it, take a few seconds to imagine what you are reading is happening. Feel your grandchild's arms around your neck... imagine looking at yourself in a mirror and admiring your thin, sexy body... or being called in for a promotion at work. In other words, allow the thoughts to bring you a sense of happiness *on the spot*.

Step 6

For the next 30 days, read "My 30-Day Commitment to Happiness" (on the following page) at least twice a day, preferably in the morning and evening. To "forget" to read these statements actually makes a statement: *I do not really want to be happy.* (This is fine, of course, and should bring a certain degree of satisfaction because what you do not want, you do not have.)

My 30-Day Commitment to Happiness

- For 30 days, I will take a vacation from the pain of my past and let it take care of itself.

- For 30 days, I will accept responsibility for all my feelings. I will blame no one, no circumstance, and no condition for the way I feel and behave.

- For 30 days, I will accept no responsibility for another adult's feelings, circumstances, or conditions.

- For 30 days, I will not judge nor criticize anyone or anything, including myself.

- For 30 days, I will be unconcerned about what others think of me. They may think what they choose. I can't stop them anyway.

- For 30 days, I will refrain from mentioning my troubles or unhappiness to anyone. I will talk about only what makes me happy.

- For 30 days, I will make no sacrifices. Others (with the exception of small children) must look after their own well-being. I have spent a lifetime attempting to help, and everyone is just as unhappy as they ever were. I deserve a break, and for 30 days, I am taking one.

- For 30 days, if I cannot watch TV or read the paper or visit with others without making judgments and feeling depressed, angry, or unhappy, I will not do these things.

- For 30 days, when I am tempted to feel selfish and guilty for being happy when others are not, I will remind myself that my unhappiness will not make them happy. Then, I will do something that makes me happy.

- For 30 days, I will look for love everywhere. I will search for it in every person, situation, and circumstance. Where I cannot identify it, I will say, "I know love must be here. If I do not see it, that does not mean it is not here." For 30 days I will allow myself to feel good about the idea that within every situation love can be found.

Step 7

(To be done every day for 30 days.)

Set aside 15 minutes to grow quiet and let your mind dwell on the idea that love is power, and love is within you. Love is within your mind; it is helping to keep your body functioning; it is given to others every time you smile or speak kindly, and it is now changing your life for the better.

If feelings of sadness or regret arise, you have unknowingly made some judgment, such as: love is gone... love is not possible for you... or you don't deserve love, etc. In other words, you have actually connected the idea of love with the idea of loss or pain, and not kept the true meaning of love in mind. Do not grow impatient with yourself. Simply dismiss the judgments, the ideas of loss, and for 15 minutes dwell on the idea that love is everywhere, within everyone—including you—and it is the most powerful force in the universe.

Let your mind consider all the ways love is powerful. Consider the bonds it creates and how it overflows into everything you do, from the care of your home, children, and pets, to the joy you feel when you are doing work you love. You want to be extremely familiar with all that love does, and know how to recognize it in every situation, because love is the power that will assist in taking you where you want to go.

Step 8

With every unpleasant encounter, think to yourself: "People are doing the best they can—including me." And let go of the unpleasant feelings that came with the encounter. If you do not let go of the unpleasant feelings immediately, repeat the thought again and add another: "I have a choice in my response."

Step 9

(Begin the fourth week.)

This exercise should be started the fourth week because for many people, it would seem unreasonably difficult if begun sooner. However, after three weeks of mental preparation, it becomes acceptable to even the hard-core "miserable." This step allows you to "practice loving" on a daily basis.

Exercise for practicing love.

During the day, with every person you encounter, regardless of how casual or fleeting, think to yourself without judgment, "I love you." Do not allow yourself to be dissuaded by self-criticism, such as, "I don't even know that person." Of course, you do. That person is like you. That person wants to love and be loved. That person may be experiencing all the anxieties that thinking of fear produces. However, not wanting to even think the words "I love you" is a thought prompted by guilt or fear.

What guilt or fear could stop you from thinking a loving thought, if love is the feeling you desire? Also, what guilt or fear could keep you from wanting to share love, except a judgmental thought that you, or the other person, is unworthy of love?

As you think, you experience. This, of course, is the benefit of this exercise. By thinking "I love you" to everyone you meet, you immediately experience the beneficial effects of the thought. You begin to feel lovable and loved.

Especially when involved in an unpleasant or angry situation, think, "I love you, and somewhere beneath our fears, I know you love me, too." This is the way to maintain a loving perspective in even the most difficult circumstance. The rewards realized from a more loving perspective cannot be overstated. Begin the exercise as soon as it seems reasonable to do so, and certainly no later than the fourth week.

Step 10

(To be done between the first and fourth weeks.)

Decide what you want to change about your life. Write it down, create a realistic plan to accomplish it, and set a realistic date for having it accomplished. Then, list five things you can do to begin, and do those things. When one item is completed, mark it off and add another. Write a positive statement—an affirmation—declaring that you will succeed. Such a statement encourages you, and helps you stay focused.

Again, the steps are:

- Decide what you want.

- Write an affirmative statement describing it.

- Decide what you must do to accomplish it.

- List what you must do.

- Set a date for its accomplishment.

- Write an affirmation.

- Each day, mark off the things you have accomplished and add another, until your goal is met.

Let's assume that your goal is to finish your education, and you know that if you apply yourself, you can do it within 18 months. Your goal-setting plan might look like this:

My Goal

I will finish my education within the next 18 months. I will accomplish this by doing the following things.

1. Talk to a school counselor.

2. Apply for a school loan.

3. Establish a schedule of night classes.

4. Awaken early to study before going to work.

5. Give my family quality time on non-class evenings and weekends.

Daily Affirmation: *I will do this because it will make me happy, and to prove that I have control of my life.*

If your goal is to lose 30 pounds, your goal-setting plan might look like this:

My Goal

I will lose 30 pounds. I will do this sensibly by losing two or three pounds a week. By (date) I will weigh _pounds. I will accomplish this by doing the following:

1. Follow a sensible diet.

2. Exercise at least 30 minutes a day.

3. Prepare and take my lunch to work.

4. Encourage myself with positive affirmations.

5. I will eat only to satisfy *physical* hunger.

Daily Affirmation: *I will do this because it will make me happy, and to prove I am in control of my life.*

The goal-setting format is simple, and it works. It is effective, even in cases where you must keep doing more and more things to accomplish your goal—such as trying to find employment in a depressed area. In such a case, the daily affirmations will be more helpful than you can imagine. They will keep your attitude positive when you would otherwise be tempted to quit.

You are always free to write your own affirmations. You are the only person who knows exactly where you need encouragement. For instance, in trying to locate a job when unemployment is high, you will need to think creatively. A good affirmation in this circumstance would be: *I am keenly alert to all possibilities and see creative solutions in all situations.*

No one has more influence in your life than you. Never pass up an opportunity to encourage yourself.

Once you have succeeded in meeting your various goals, you can reflect on all the abusive memories that you thought were holding you back, and see that they weren't. Memories have power only when you are willing to give them power, which means, *when you think about them.* Thinking about anything gives that idea life and power.

Use the following form to assist you until you memorize the formula.

GOAL FOCUSING STATEMENT

My present goal is: _____

I will make it a reality by this date: _____

What I can do to make it happen:

1. _____

2. _____

3. _____

4. _____

5. _____

Affirm: *I will work from this list every day until I make my goal a reality. I will waste no time or energy blaming others for what "goes wrong." I will use my mind effectively to meet my goal.*

As you work The Option

Do not be discouraged if, at first, you find old thought patterns inundating you at every turn. This is to be expected. This is subconscious resistance generated by old beliefs that *(1) you do not deserve to be happy, and (2) your suffering is "proof" that you have nothing to do with the pain you're experiencing.*

Be willing to challenge these erroneous ideas for at least 30 days.

As old and painful thoughts come to mind, stop them as soon as you become aware of them, and choose a happy thought. The only reason you hesitate to do this is that you have accepted a belief that you are not "good enough" to deserve happiness. Do it anyway. If you wait until you feel "good enough," you will never be happy. It is not possible to start loving yourself until you begin doing loving things for yourself, and thinking loving thoughts *is* doing something loving.

Keep in mind that reprimanding yourself for having made mistakes is to continue making a mistake.

In only 30 days, it is possible to experience the true power of love and to recognize that you are in control of your life—your happiness, love, success, and prosperity. If, after

30 days, you want to change your mind and feel guilty or unhappy again, you are certainly free to do so.

The power of love that helps you overcome the effects of painful experiences is eternal. It cannot be taken from you, but you can forget you have it. Love cannot be felt until it is given away—and with every thought you think, you are "giving" either love or fear to yourself and everyone around you.

Love will always rescue you if you remember to use it, but it cannot rescue you if you choose to remember pain and fear.

God is love. Love is always with you and willing to help if you remember to think loving thoughts.

Tips to remember:

The past cannot hurt you unless you choose to remember it.

Memories have no power over you; they cannot alter your decision.

Every thought creates a corresponding emotion—so think encouraging thoughts!

There are two thought categories: love and fear. Thoughts that make you happy and create a sense of well-being are loving thoughts. Thoughts that hurt and create doubt are fear-based and will undermine your success.

You have a choice between thoughts. Choose wisely.

You cannot control others, situations, circumstances, the past, or the future—nor do you need to. You only need to control your responses to them.

Pain is an effect created by something that has already happened. What has happened is in the past. All pain is in the past unless you bring it into our present thoughts.

Present thoughts of past pain create present pain.

Fear is created by thinking of something that might happen in the future. Fear cannot exist in the present unless you are presently thinking fearful thoughts.

Fearful thoughts will immobilize you. Replace them immediately with encouraging thoughts.

What you believe creates the reality you experience.

Denying yourself happiness does not make you "good," it makes you and everyone around you miserable.

Ever-Present Help

There is a Power within you that is sufficient to overcome all obstacles. It doesn't care what you call It, but It is there and It responds to love—your loving thoughts, your loving your life, your loving others, your loving your dreams and pursuing them.

If you will remember to love your life, family, friends, the day, your work—love will empower you, and soon you will love all that you have accomplished.

You will also love the truth that you—and only you—control your life. Love gives you that control.

Last Minute Advice

Creating each list in this mental program is necessary for your success. While the lists are tedious, they are also essential. Don't be tempted to believe that *understanding the concept* is sufficient. The lists provide enlightenment and fortify your commitment, helping you succeed.

Notes and Affirmations

_____

_____

_____

_____

_____

_____

_____

_____

_____

_____

_____

_____

_____

_____

_____

_____

_____

_____

_____

_____

_____

_____

_____

_____

_____

_____

_____

_____

_____

_____

_____

_____

_____

_____

OTHER SPIRITUAL AND NONFICTION BOOKS
BY OTHELLO BACH

Cry Into the Wind
Angel Within
101 Questions for God
The Father Within
Body Designing
Secrets of Successful Writers
How to Write a Great Story

Othello is a bestselling multi-genre author of numerous books which range in scope and variety from suspense novels, children's books, spiritual books, to non-fiction "How-to" books. Her memoir "Cry into the Wind," chronicles an abusive childhood, including 11 years in an orphanage.

Although a non-reader until the eighth grade, she wrote and sold her first novel to Avon Books when she was 24.

Othello often composes music and lyrics to accompany her children's stories, and celebrities Joel Grey, Tammy Grimes and Sandy Duncan have recorded her books and songs.

She is a motivational speaker who loves to share "the tools" that helped her overcome an abusive past.

Othello Bach